MORAL OR LESS

By Maxine Nodel

Music composed by
Deborah Nodel Gordon
Illustrations by
Norman Nodel

MORAL OR LESS

FIRST EDITION
First Impression — APRIL 1990

Published by HaChai Publishing

Copyright © 1990 by HaChai Publishing
ALL RIGHTS RESERVED

This book, or parts thereof, may not be reproduced, stored, or copied in any form without written permission from the copyright holder, except by a reviewer who wishes to quote brief passages in connection with a review written for inclusion in magazines or newspapers.

THE RIGHTS OF THE COPYRIGHT HOLDER
WILL BE STRICTLY ENFORCED.

ISBN 0—922613—25—7 (Casebound Edition)
ISBN 0—922613—26—5 (Softcover Edition)
ISBN 0—922613—27—3 (Workbook Edition)
ISBN 0—922613—28—1 (Audio Cassette)

Distributed by:
HaChai Distributions
705 Foster Avenue
Brooklyn, New York 11230
(718) 692-3900

Printed in Hong Kong

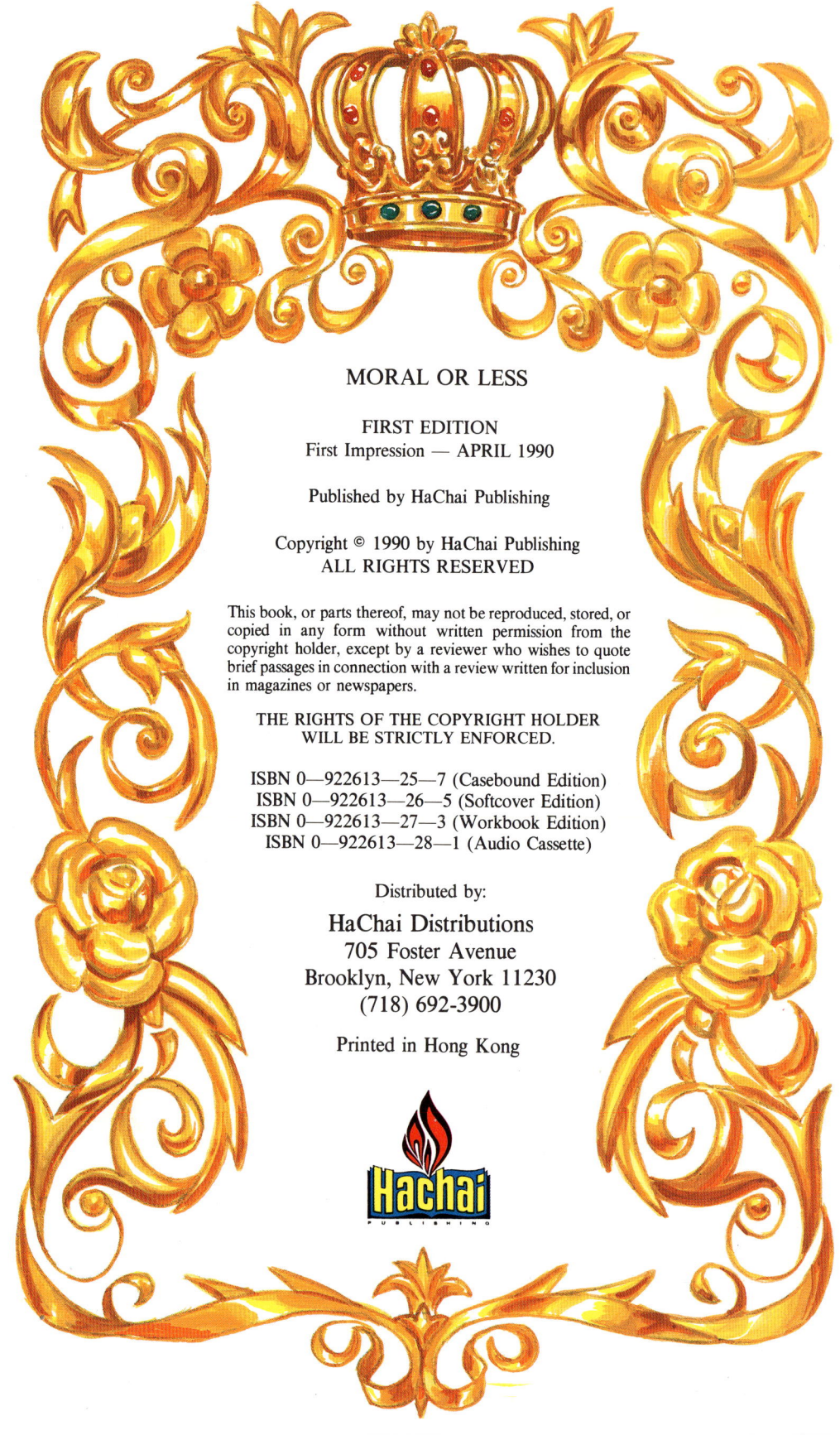

Moral Or Less

Some time ago in a place near you,
Lived a very good and pious Jew.
He followed the commandments faithfully,
And taught his children diligently.

Not only he, but his wife did too,
She taught each child to be a good Jew.

Their children, named Dina and Dovid,
Honored their parents and gave them much *kovid*.

But something odd happened that month of Iyar,
It was on Lag B'Omer and rather bizarre!

Dina and Dovid bubbled with cheer,
The Lag B'Omer picnic was almost here.
They jumped for joy, for to their surprise,
Abba and Imma packed picnic supplies.

"Children," said Imma, "are you both delighted?"
"A trip to the woods? We're very excited!"
But Dovid stopped cheering. "I just don't feel swell.
Look at my math test; I didn't do well.

I tried and I tried, but I just cannot add!"
Imma said, "Now isn't time to be sad!
I'll help you tonight, when the picnic is done,
Now go with your class,
                          and please have some fun."

"Why celebrate Lag B'Omer this way?"
Said Dina to Abba. "What's this holiday?"
"Sit down," said Abba, "and I'll tell you why.
In Rabbi Shimon's lifetime,
                          no rainbows were high.
But Hashem did honor this man of great worth,
With a rainbow on his last day on earth.

A rainbow appeared on that memorable day
Of Lag B'Omer, when he passed away.
Because on this day he taught all he could find,
He taught them all Torah from his heart and his mind.
He prayed that this day be a time of great joy,
A day to remember by each girl and boy.

The bow in the sky tells of Jews who were bold,
When Romans ruled Israel, in days of old.
There was a big rainbow way up in the sky
On Rabbi Shimon's last day on earth.
Hashem did honor this man of great worth.
The bow in the sky meant another sad time,
When the Romans ruled Israel, in old Palestine.

They didn't permit it
    when Torah was taught,
And punished severely
    the Jews who were caught.
But Rabbi Akiva
    continued to teach,
He taught every Jew
    he was able to reach.

'Jews without Torah are fish without water!
Continue to study!' was the rabbi's strict order."

"How did they study? Did they wear a disguise?"
Asked Dina aloud, with sudden surprise.
Imma said, "Yes, they went in the woods,
They took bows and arrows and all hunting goods.
And there in the woods they would study in fear,
Knowing the Romans could be very near!

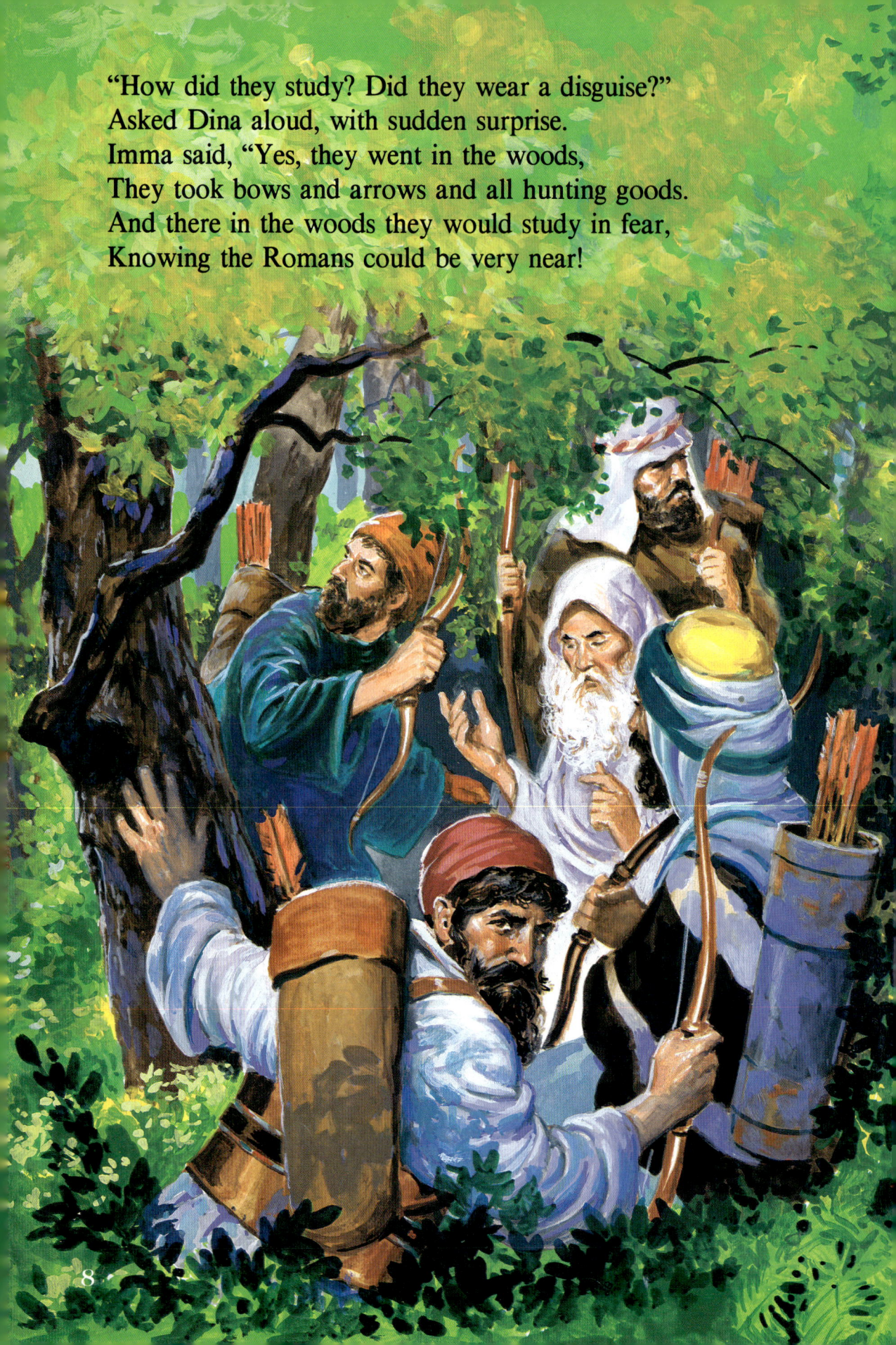

Then there were times when they hid in a cave,
Studying Torah, fearful but brave."

So Dina and Dovid went with their class,
Into the woods and tumbled on grass.
The children divided and hid behind trees,
They crawled with their arrows and walked on their knees.
They played and they played and hid behind rocks,
Some of the children took off their socks.
Dovid did try to have the same fun,
But thought of his math test and sat in the sun.

Soon the blue sky began to turn dark,
And Dovid looked 'round the large wooded park.
He didn't see Dina! He looked for his class!
He stood still and yelled, "Which tree did I pass?"

Then all of a sudden, in a white flash of light,
As if a star came from the darkness of night,
Appeared a small man. He held a math book.
And Dovid blinked twice with a large blue-eyed look.
"Are you thinking of math?" said the man with a smile.
"I love working numbers. It's been a long while."

"But who might you be and why are you here?"
The man came closer. "You've nothing to fear.
I'm the Math Maven and I make things click,
We're going to do *arhy-thmetic!*
I always appear when I hear a math thought,
And I know Addition is what you were taught."

"It's the Lag B'Omer picnic and I cannot have fun."
"Why?" asked the Maven. "'Cause you can't find a sum?
I think I can teach you Addition today,
You can learn to add on this great holiday!"

"Through Lag B'Omer we'll do addition?"
"Yes," said the Maven. "But there's one condition.
Give me your word; when you learn to add:
Don't become greedy and make people sad.
For when you add numbers, you always get more,
And more is what people will always adore."

"I won't!" Dovid said. "I can sure tell you that!"
Then on the green grass the Math Maven sat.

"Sum, Add, Total,
and the word Plus,
All mean Addition.
There's more to discuss.
We'll take some numbers
and try to find the sum,
Put them in a column
and soon you'll be done.
When they're lined up
you're ready to proceed.
The One's place now
is the place that you need.
That's at the right,
now begin to add down.
Count everything towards
the grass on the ground.

When you are finished
just see what you've got.
If it's only one digit
then write it on the spot.
But a two-digit number?
Please don't assume!
Just Two is written down,
there isn't any room.

The One says, 'Bye,'
and now has gone,
Up to the Ten's place,
then adds itself on.
You'll have Thirty-two,
and that's that with that."
Then the Maven vanished
from the place that he sat.

Dovid called the Maven
but he just wasn't there.
It seemed as if the Maven
disappeared into thin air.
"I didn't even thank him,"
said Dovid with a frown.
"But now I know Addition,
I'll tell everyone in town."
Dovid started walking
and looking all around,
The sky was getting darker,
he saw something near the ground.
It glistened! It was small,
and was lying near a stone,
Dovid moved to see the strange
golden thing that shone.

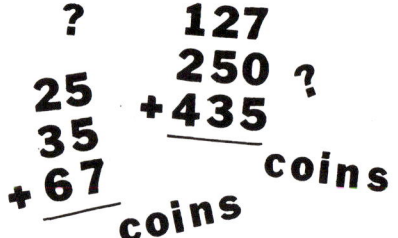

"It looks just like a coin,
but not one I've ever seen."
He brushed the dirt from its face
until the coin was clean.
He put it in his pocket
and walked past all the trees,
Then he saw more gold coins
right below his knees.
"I'll be rich!" Dovid said,
collecting up his find,
He put the gold in his palm
and did math in his mind.
He continued on his journey,
thinking how much he could save,
Soon it rained and he was cold,
just then he saw a cave.

He walked into the darkness
and wandered towards the back,
In the dim yellow light
he saw a small brown sack.
He opened it quite slowly,
then Dovid, being bold,
Put his fingers in the bag
and pulled out coins of gold.
He put them in his pockets
and then he heard some talking,

He turned his head towards the sound
and saw a Roman walking!

"Let's see all our shekels,
the ones we took from Jews!"
On hearing this Dovid shook
and dropped coins on his shoes.

"What was that?" the Roman said,
running towards the sound,
Dovid could not run away,
his foot stuck to the ground!
For all the gold he stuffed
into the pockets of his shirt,
Made it so he could not move
his body from the dirt.
The Roman was approaching
and Dovid tried to move,
Then a voice behind him said,
"Of this I don't approve!"

Dovid turned to see the man,
he looked with great surprise.
"Are you Dovid?" said the man.
"You haven't been so wise."

"I thought the gold would bring me joy!"
said Dovid with a frown.
He took the shekels from his clothes
and threw them on the ground.

At that moment Dovid felt much lighter than before,
Then hand in hand they flew away above the rocky floor!

Before Dovid knew it
he was in another cave,
He saw some Jewish boys
who looked so proud and brave.
The boys looked up at Dovid,
and then they saw the man.
"Shalom, Rabbi Akiva!"
said a boy with scroll in hand.

"The scrolls the boys are holding
are words worth more than gold,
They are the words of Hashem,
and through the Torah told!

Add Torah to your heart and mind,
your mitzvos will increase.
Subtract the greed that's in your soul,
your problems will decrease!"

Dovid said, "I know that when I learned to add
I did a greedy act.
But now I'll take the greed away,
I must learn to subtract!"

All of a sudden, in a white flash of light,
As if a star came from the darkness of night,
Appeared the Math Maven, with numbers galore.
"I told you that more is what people adore.

So listen to me and you'll soon take away,
We'll do subtraction, you'll learn it today.
Subtraction, you see, will make your day,
Instead of adding you just take away.

Like with Addition,
you start from the right,
But don't go so fast,
like the speed of light.

The number you take from,
is it too small?
You'll have to borrow,
you must recall!

If you take a Six
from the number Three,
Borrow from the Ten's place,
it's easy, you see.

If you borrow from a Five,
it then becomes Four.

Take the little One, fast,
and now there is more!

You took from the Five,
here taking isn't mean,
The Three is happy
and becomes Thirteen.
The Six can be taken away from its number,
You'll have Seventeen,
are you ready for slumber?"

Dovid rubbed his eyes,
and then he was alone,
He stretched and yawned, then fell asleep
on soft grass near a stone.

"Dovid, Dovid, please wake up,
it's time for us to leave."
Dovid opened both his eyes
and rubbed them with his sleeve.

Dina said, "Where were you?
It's getting very dark.
It's time for us to leave now,
they're closing up the park."

So Dina and Dovid were back home at last,
He told everyone of all that had passed.
"What a wonderful dream!" his parents both said.
And then Imma smiled. "It's time now for bed."
Abba said, "Do you need help with your math?"
"No, thank you, Abba, I'm taking a bath."

He walked to his room and pulled down the cover,
And to his surprise, what did he discover?
There on his pillow were coins, gold and bright.
"I'd love to keep them, but I know that's not right.

I understand now it's not right to be greedy,
I must think of others and give to the needy.
I'll take them and give them all to the poor,
I'll add to the *pushka* that hangs on my door."